GROW YOUR PRODUCT BUSINESS

Based on *Tame Your Tiger* by
Catherine Erdly

First published in Great Britain by Practical Inspiration Publishing, 2026

© Catherine Erdly and Practical Inspiration Publishing, 2026

The moral rights of the author have been asserted

ISBN 978-1-78860-895-4   (paperback)
      978-1-78860-896-1   (ebook)

All rights reserved. This book, or any portion thereof, may not be reproduced without the express written permission of the publisher.

Every effort has been made to trace copyright holders and to obtain their permission for the use of copyright material. The publisher apologizes for any errors or omissions and would be grateful if notified of any corrections that should be incorporated in future reprints or editions of this book.

EU GPSR representative: LOGOS EUROPE, 9 rue Nicolas Poussin, LA ROCHELLE 17000, France Contact@logoseurope.eu.

Want to bulk-buy copies of this book for your team and colleagues? We can customize the content and co-brand *Grow Your Product Business* to suit your business's needs.

Please email info@practicalinspiration.com for more details.

Contents

Series introduction iv

Introduction 1

Day 1: Where's the money going? 5

Day 2: What does it really cost to sell? 15

Day 3: What's left after the sale? 27

Day 4: Is your stock helping or hurting? 37

Day 5: How much stock do you actually
need? 45

Day 6: What does it cost to stay open? 53

Day 7: How can you grow without
burning out? 64

Day 8: Are you charging enough? 74

Day 9: How do you fix slim margins? 83

Day 10: What's next? 92

Conclusion 101

Series introduction

Welcome to *6-Minute Smarts*!

This is a series of very short books with one simple purpose: to introduce you to ideas that can make life and work better, and to give you time and space to think about how those ideas might apply to *your* life and work.

Each book introduces you to ten powerful ideas, but ideas on their own are useless – that's why each idea is followed by self-coaching questions to help you work out the 'so what?' for you in just six minutes of exploratory writing. What's exploratory writing? It's the kind of writing you do just for yourself, fast and free, without worrying what anyone else thinks. It's not just about getting ideas out of your head and onto paper where you can see them; it's about finding new connections and insights as you write. This is where the magic happens.

Whatever you're facing, there's a *6-Minute Smarts* book just for you. And once you've learned how to coach yourself through a new idea, you'll be smarter for life.

Find out more...

Introduction

Imagine this. One day you see an adorable stripy ball of fur and can't resist taking it home. You feed it, love it, constantly think of ways to improve its life and care for it. Then one day, after you find yourself yet again trying to figure out what this creature wants, you realize that instead of a tame tabby cat, you are actually the owner of a fully grown tiger.

Product businesses are like that. They seem incredibly appealing when you are first starting out; then, before you know it, you are at the deep end trying to figure out what on earth to do.

How do you know if you have a tiger in your business? The easiest way to understand this is to think about how your business makes you feel.

Do any of the following sound familiar?

- You feel constantly on the back foot and your business seems unpredictable.
- You wonder if you are out of your depth.
- There doesn't seem to be enough money to get the help you need.
- As you grow and get busier, you seem to be doing more and more instead of being able to step away.
- The business seems to be demanding increasing amounts of money so as soon as you have sales coming in, money is going straight out again to cover stock or other expenses.

Tigers feel scary as we aren't trained to recognize or manage them. But growing sales alone – without understanding and managing these other elements – is not enough to alleviate financial stress in your business.

The three areas we need to look at and measure are:

- the teeth – how big of a bite is being taken out of our sales;
- the tail – how much unproductive stock is trapped in our business;
- the stomach – how much we are feeding the beast.

Introduction

This is the world that I was immersed in for nearly two decades. A world that is highly governed by the numbers, with profitability kept in sharp focus.

While I vastly prefer working with small and medium-sized businesses, and find the passion, energy and innovation of this sector of the retail industry highly motivating, there are some aspects of the way that bigger businesses are run that small businesses could benefit from.

That's what I aim to do with this book. I want to take some of those big business learnings and help you apply them to your small business. The combination of small business passion and big business discipline is a powerful recipe for success.

We'll be using a series of fictionalized case studies to examine the issues more closely. Everything in this book is drawing on my experience of more than two decades in the retail industry.

The book is applicable to different models of product businesses, whether you have a bricks and mortar shop, an e-commerce store or a mixture of both. The principles will be relevant whether you make the products you sell or curate them from other businesses, and whether you sell through your own website, someone else's website or directly to the public. Ultimately, if you sell products to people, this book is for you.

Right now you might feel unsure of yourself or frustrated with your inability to manage your business. A common phenomenon is something I call 'the hot flush of shame'. It's that feeling you get when you think you should know certain numbers or facts about your business. But you never take the time to look because you don't know where to start or even why these numbers are important.

You probably feel overwhelmed, wondering if you will ever work out how to make money. Some successes come your way but even as your sales grow, you feel stuck and unsure about how or why these sales successes are not translating into profitability, or why your profitability is lower than before.

Without a solid understanding of what numbers you should be aiming for, you can feel a little bit lost. What's more, even if you do set yourself goals, you don't know what actions to take if you are not hitting or exceeding your goals.

But if you're ready to feel more in control of your numbers, get clear about what you want to be measuring and become more confident about managing your tiger – let's go!

Day 1
Where's the money going?

Trying to solve a tiger problem just by selling more is a common trap. But it can actually make things worse.

Growing sales means more people to employ, more storage space or bigger facilities, more packaging, more stock. If you are under-profitable with small sales, as you grow that won't change. Without visibility of key numbers, sleepwalking into lower profits is a real possibility.

Similarly with the stock issue, unless you keep an eye on that tail as you grow, it will also grow along with you. And remember, the bigger the tail, the bigger the tiger. I've worked with several fast-growth businesses who haven't paid close enough attention to their amount of stock, causing a major problem as sales increased.

Yes, more sales is a very important part of growing and developing your business. However, as we'll see later, it's only part of the story.

It's entirely possible to have a six-figure, or even a seven-, eight-, nine- or ten-figure product business that makes *no* money. Believe me, I've worked with, or for, several. But here's the good news – the more you learn and practise these principles, the more well equipped you'll be as your business grows to understand the pressures, the pain points and, ultimately, how to keep that tiger under control.

There are three places in your business that you can look at to help you tame your tiger.

The teeth

How big of a bite is taken out of your revenue with each sale?

If you sell an item for £12, and after tax and expenses are left with £7.50, your business is going to feel very different to one where there is only £2.50 left. Understanding what that looks like for your business and how to manage and measure it will go a long way.

The tail

This is the name given in retail to the unproductive stock in your business. The 80/20 rule applies: 80% of your sales will come from 20% of your products. The other 80%? That's your tail. And having too much of it is one of the quickest ways to lock up cash and create a tiger.

The stomach

How much are you feeding the beast? If your business has too many fixed expenses – staffing, agency fees or premises – it is very difficult to grow profitably.

To give more context to these concepts, I'm going to introduce you to three fictionalized characters.

Each character is entirely made up (and any resemblance to any real-life people or businesses is entirely coincidental), but they are an amalgamation of hundreds of conversations I've had over the years with product businesses of all sizes.

The case studies are three small snapshots into different types of product businesses – an independent bricks and mortar store, a small e-commerce store and a larger business selling via the web and wholesale.

They bring to life some of the common issues and challenges outlined in the book, and if you recognize what they are talking about pay particular attention to their story to see whether or not your tiger has some of the same characteristics as theirs. Let's meet them now.

Salma the shop owner

Salma has always dreamed of having her own shop. After taking voluntary redundancy, she opened her dream boutique in her home town in 2019. She loves being part of the local community, as well as everything to do with the creative side of running the shop. What Salma is not so fond of is balancing her numbers every month. With members of staff to pay, and rent, rates and increasingly expensive utilities to cover each month, she has a lot to manage.

> We have a lot of local artists who stock with us on a 'sale or return' basis. In theory, this is ideal because it means we don't pay to have the stock in the store; we only pay when it sells. In reality, at the end of each month, I always have to pay an amount of money out of my sales to the sale or return artists, which never seems to leave enough for me. I feel like I'm on

Where's the money going?

a treadmill. As soon as money comes in, it just goes straight out again.

Emmanuel the e-commerce seller

Emmanuel has a degree in product design, but after university took a job working in the civil service. His passion for design never left him though, and he started a blog about creating a design-led home as a hobby. Over the years, he started to add some links to the blog to allow readers to purchase certain products from different websites. One day he realized that he could sell them himself. He switched the blog to a shoppable platform and started with a small range of highly curated products, eventually having a small range of products manufactured for him as well. Emmanuel now has about 100 products on his site, including the items that he manufactures, as well as pieces from other businesses. He has recently moved to a fulfilment centre, finally getting his living room back!

> I have to place large orders at a time for each of my products, which means that I have to tie up a lot of cash at the same time. That used to be OK, but now that I'm VAT registered and I have the fulfilment centre, it

feels like I'm making less and less on each item. Sometimes I feel like I'm having a good month and then end up having some real problems with my cash flow. Other times it feels a bit quieter but I am covering my costs. I feel like I'm winging it most of the time.

Irene the illustrator

Irene spent 17 years in marketing, before a health scare made her re-evaluate her stressful job. With two small children and a wife who worked full time, they made the decision that Irene would leave her job and stay at home to help create more of a balance for the whole family. Once her youngest child was at nursery, she started to think about ways that she could contribute to the family finances doing something she loved. She began painting beautiful artwork for her friends' nurseries. They were so popular that she decided to open up an Etsy shop with prints of her artwork and cards, as well as taking a stall on her local craft market. After a couple of years where sales rose steadily, Irene decided to wholesale her prints and cards and now has around 40 stockists. She still sells via Etsy but mostly drives traffic to her Shopify website.

Where's the money going?

Recently, with more and more expenses in my business, from the studio to the team members and the costs associated with those, I have found myself increasingly worried about the profit. If I have even one quiet day, I immediately start asking myself whether I'm going to have enough money to cover all of my expenses. I can't quite seem to get a handle on what my sales need to be for the new costs that I have. I thought it would get easier the more that I grow, but I feel way more stressed than I was at the beginning when it was just me and my paintbrush.

Although each of these business owners has a different model and way of selling their products, they all share some of the same characteristics of a tiger business – nervousness, uncertainty about what to do for the best and lack of visibility around how to make the next best move.

Before we look at how to address *all* of these issues, take a moment to reflect on where you're at right now.

So what? Over to you…

1. Have you fallen into the trap of simply trying to sell more stock in the past? What happened?

Where's the money going?

2. Do you recognize any of the descriptions of how tiger businesses make you feel?

3. Do any of the stories from Salma, Emmanuel and Irene sound familiar? What parts do you relate to?

Day 2
What does it really cost to sell?

What does it really cost you every time you make a sale? Many product business owners are unsure of the answer – and as a result, they have no clear idea whether the business is profitable or why the profits are smaller than expected. Day 2 is all about truly understanding the tiger's top teeth, your profit margin: what you buy an item for compared to what you sell it for.

It can be tempting to focus only on how much money comes in, but the reality is that sales are only half the story. Consider this:

There is only one place in your business that you generate money – the difference between what you pay for your stock and what you sell it for.

Every cost that you have in your business, including your rent, advertising, staff costs, the salary you want to pay yourself or anything else that you can think of, has to be covered by the difference between what you pay to buy or make your products and what you sell them for.

One of the biggest differences between successful retailers and those that struggle is their grasp of profit margins. A retailer with a clear understanding of how much money they make on every sale is in a much better position to spot problems, adjust prices and make good decisions about what to sell next.

If your topline revenue grows without enough attention to what is happening with your profits, it's entirely possible to have a business with a large and growing turnover that isn't making any money.

In-margin

The 'in-margin' is a hypothetical figure that doesn't appear on any accounting report: it relates to the relationship between your cost price and planned

What does it really cost to sell?

selling price (the 'out-margin' looks at your cost price and what you actually sold something for, taking into account any discounts).

The price that you pay for a product compared to the price that you are planning on selling it for is your in-margin.

When you know your in-margin, you know how much money you should have left over from each sale to contribute toward your other costs, like your own salary, rent or marketing.

For example, if you price a mug at £12, but it costs you £5 to buy, £1 for packaging and £0.50 in payment fees, your in-margin is:

£12 (price) − £5 (cost) − £1 (packaging) − £0.50 (fees) = £5.50.

Many business owners stop after calculating the cost of buying or making the product, but don't include all those extra small costs that add up over time. When you do include them, you might be surprised at how much less you're actually making.

One hidden cost that many UK business owners forget is VAT. (Remember: always speak with your accountant about anything tax related, so that you can be sure to get tailored advice specific to your unique situation.) But in broad terms, if you're VAT registered, the VAT you collect is not your money – it belongs to the government. If you're not careful, it's easy to accidentally spend that money and then face a nasty shock at the end of the quarter.

When you look at your in-margin, always calculate it after VAT if you're registered. If you're not yet VAT registered, keep in mind that your margins will take a dip when you do cross the threshold – although the impact may be partially offset because any VAT that you are paying on your supplies will net off against the VAT from sales.

Common mistakes in calculating in-margin

1. Not including all the direct costs (postage, packaging, fees, VAT).
2. Calculating margin only as a percentage, not as a cash amount per item.
3. Focusing on 'bestsellers' by volume rather than by total profit generated.

The 80/20 rule applies here: it's common for 20% of your products to bring in 80% of your profits. The rest may tie up time and cash without delivering much value.

What does it really cost to sell?

Case study: Salma reviews her in-margin

I decided to work through all of the products in my business to see what kind of margins I was getting.

For the items that I bought upfront on wholesale, I found that generally those margins were right around the 50% mark. The cost of some other items in the shop had increased more than 20% since I first started buying them, but I hadn't increased any of my prices to reflect that, even though when I checked I discovered that the manufacturer's RRP had increased.

The other element to factor in is that around 50% of my sales are coming from the sale or return items, which have at most a 25% margin.

This means that, on average, I'm only achieving around a 37.5% in-margin across the whole business. No wonder it feels tight.

I decided to start with a full review of all of my pricing from my wholesale items, making sure that I was, at the very least, using the most up-to-date RRPs.

Next up, I ran through the profit margins on each product and considered whether or not to keep stocking the ones that were below a 50% margin.

There are three best-selling items that come from the same supplier so I decided to have a conversation with them about the pricing. I explained that I was trying to grow my profitability and that I needed to do better with the pricing. I asked them what it would take for me to get these items at £6 instead of the £7.50 I was paying at the moment, and they suggested that if I spent at least £500 when I placed an order with them, they could offer me a 10% discount. I was happy with that.

For the sale or return items, I approached the top three makers to ask them if they would wholesale me the items instead. One of them absolutely cannot do wholesale pricing, so I'm going to have to keep them as sale or return, but the other two were open to making the switch, especially since it meant that they would be paid upfront.

I also took a look at some of the makers where I hadn't sold anything for a few months and made arrangements to return their stock. Removing the unproductive sale-or-return stock from the shelf has helped me feel more in control and positive, and I've also had a few nice comments from customers about the shop feeling more airy and easy to browse in.

What does it really cost to sell?

Practical exercise

Take a sheet of paper or open a spreadsheet and list your top ten products. For each one, write down:

- Sale price
- Cost of product
- Cost of packaging
- Shipping costs (if you cover them)
- Payment or platform fees
- VAT (if applicable).

Subtract all these from the sale price to get your in-margin per item.

Do this for your top sellers and compare – which ones give you the best return? Which are not as profitable as you thought?

If you find that your margins are thin across the board, ask yourself:

- Can I negotiate better terms with suppliers?
- Can I increase prices, even slightly?
- Are there cheaper packaging or shipping options?
- Is there a way to bundle products for better margin?

Many small business owners worry that increasing prices will scare customers away, but in reality customers don't always notice small price increases, especially if you communicate the value they're getting. It's more damaging to your business to undercharge than it is to lose a few price-sensitive customers.

It's also important to regularly review your prices as your own costs change. Cost prices have increased across almost every category over the last few years. If you haven't reviewed your prices recently, now is the time.

Out-margin

If the in-margin represents how much money you would sell an item for if you sold it at full price, which is looking forward into the future, the out-margin, or gross profit margin, is an analysis of historical sales data to show what actually happened.

Here's a simplified model for calculating your gross profit margin for a product:

Gross profit margin = (Actual sale price − Direct costs) / Actual sale price × 100%

What does it really cost to sell?

If you sell something priced at £25 for £20 and your direct costs are £8, your out-margin/gross profit margin is: (£20 − £8) / £20 x 100% = 60%

Industry standards vary, but many small retailers aim for at least 50% gross profit margin on most products. If your average is below this, you will struggle to cover all your business costs.

The mental shift

Understanding your profit margins is empowering not limiting. When you see what you're actually making, you have the power to change it – by changing your pricing, your sourcing or your focus.

It's easy to fall into the trap of chasing turnover (total sales) and losing sight of actual profit. Remember: it's not what you sell, it's what you keep.

So what? Over to you...

1. Is your pricing right? Try checking the in-margin for your top sellers.

What does it really cost to sell?

2. How, if at all, does your out-margin differ from your in-margin for your top sellers? Why is that?

3. What's one action, however small, you can take this week to improve your out-margin?

Day 3
What's left after the sale?

It's a common story for product business owners: you're making sales, but the money never seems to stick around. At the end of each month, the bank account is emptier than you hoped, and it's not clear why. This is the reality of net profit – what's left after all the bills, costs and extras are taken care of.

The truth is, a business can have strong gross profit margins but still struggle if those profits are swallowed up by other costs. The real question isn't just 'what did I make on the sale?' but 'what's left for me after everything else?'

Understanding net profit

Once you've calculated your out-margin, or gross profit, you need to look at what happens next: the rest of your business costs. These are often called overheads, fixed costs or operating expenses. They are the things you have to pay for, whether you make one sale or one thousand.

Common examples:

- Rent or mortgage payments on your workspace
- Utilities and phone bills
- Salaries and freelancers
- Website hosting, subscriptions and apps
- Marketing and advertising
- Insurance and legal fees.

Some of these are 'fixed' – they don't change much month to month. Others are 'variable' – they go up and down with your sales. Keeping them under control is vital.

Why net profit matters

It's possible to be busy, have happy customers and still be making a loss. The money that comes in can

What's left after the sale?

be eaten away by these less visible expenses, leaving nothing for you at the end.

If you don't know what your net margin is – the profit that remains after every single cost is taken out – then you can't make smart decisions about your prices, stock or even how much to pay yourself.

Case study: Emmanuel gets a wake-up call

Emmanuel was delighted when his website's turnover hit £10,000 in a month for the first time. But after paying the fulfilment centre, ad spend, transaction fees, VAT and freelance help, his actual profit was only £420.

It wasn't until Emmanuel listed every single cost – and subtracted them from his gross profit – that he understood where the money was going. Only by seeing the full picture did he realize what he needed to change.

Net profit calculation

Start with your gross profit (sales minus direct costs). From this, subtract all your operating costs. What's left is your net profit – the money that's really yours.

Gross profit – Overheads = Net profit

For example, suppose you sell £5,000 worth of products in a month. Your direct costs (stock, packaging, fees) are £2,200, leaving a gross profit of £2,800.

Now subtract:

- Rent: £500
- Utilities: £80
- Website/app subscriptions: £60
- Marketing: £300
- Wages/freelancers: £1,200
- Insurance: £30

Total overheads: £2,170
Net profit: £2,800 − £2,170 = £630

It can be a shock to see how little is left after all expenses. Unless you monitor both gross margin and net margin, profit will always feel mysterious.

Why is my net profit margin so slim?

Several factors can shrink your net profit margin:

- Too many fixed costs, especially as the business grows
- Overcommitting to marketing, subscriptions or workspace
- Not reviewing costs regularly

What's left after the sale?

- Growing sales without reviewing overheads
- Not putting yourself on payroll (so your 'profit' isn't really profit at all!).

Note that more sales can mean more costs too: more stock, more time, more admin. Unless you know your numbers, it's possible to grow your way into bigger problems.

The monthly profit and loss snapshot

The simplest way to keep an eye on your net profit margin is to create a monthly profit and loss statement (P&L). List your sales, subtract direct costs, then subtract your other business expenses. The figure at the bottom is what you truly made.

Even a simple spreadsheet, updated at the end of every month, gives you powerful insight. If the bottom line is red (negative), you need to either grow margin or cut costs.

Practical exercise

Create a list of every recurring business expense. Are there any that could be trimmed, renegotiated or eliminated?

- Have you reviewed every subscription and software fee in the last six months?
- Are you paying for services you no longer use?

Even small changes add up.

Variable vs fixed costs

Some costs, like materials or postage, rise and fall as you sell more. Others (like rent) are fixed. During busy periods, variable costs can spike – but fixed costs can be particularly dangerous if sales slow down. It's easy to get excited by growth and add new staff, bigger studios, fancier tools, but the ideal is to keep fixed costs as low as possible, so you can weather quieter months without stress. (We'll talk more about these in Day 6.)

Cash flow and timing

Sometimes the issue isn't the net profit itself, but the timing of payments. You might be profitable 'on paper' but have no cash in the bank because bills are due before your sales money comes in.

It's vital to keep a cash flow calendar – knowing when money comes in and when it goes out – to avoid nasty surprises.

What's left after the sale?

Paying yourself

A healthy business pays the owner. If there's never anything left for you – or you're the first to skip a 'payday' when things are tight – it's time to take a closer look at your net profit margin.

Regularly reviewing your net profit margin lets you see if your business model is truly sustainable.

Remember: it's not just about working harder or selling more. Knowing your real, final profit – what's left after everything is paid – is the foundation for making good decisions, planning for growth and building a sustainable business.

If you focus only on sales, you can be busy but broke. If you focus on what's left, you can build a business that truly supports you.

So what? Over to you...

1. When was the last time you reviewed all your business expenses, line by line?

What's left after the sale?

2. Are there fixed costs you've accepted as 'just the way it is' or could you renegotiate or remove something to improve your net profit margin?

3. How do you ensure that you're on top of the cash flow in your business?

Day 4
Is your stock helping or hurting?

If you run a product business, stock is both your biggest asset and your biggest risk. It's easy to end up with too much cash tied up in stock that isn't selling – and not enough in the products your customers really want. This is the challenge of managing your 'tail' – the part of your stock that is sitting, unsold, and holding your business back.

Many business owners find themselves with overflowing shelves, drawers or storage units, yet still feel they have 'nothing to sell'. The answer lies in understanding the difference between productive and unproductive stock.

Why do businesses accumulate unproductive stock?

There are several reasons why product businesses end up with too much of the wrong stock:

- Wanting to offer customers a broad choice
- Over-ordering because of supplier minimums
- Buying in bulk for a discount
- 'Magpie syndrome' – chasing new ideas and trends
- Fear of running out and missing sales
- Reluctance to discount or get rid of old stock.

Unproductive stock is like a hidden tax on your business. You pay for it up front, then pay again to store it, count it and manage it. And every week or month it sits unsold, it gets less valuable.

The 80/20 rule (Pareto Principle)

One of the most powerful – and sobering – ideas in retail is the 80/20 rule, also known as the Pareto Principle. In a product business, it usually means that 80% of your sales come from just 20% of your products. The other 80% of your stock? That's your

Is your stock helping or hurting?

'tail'. And the bigger the tail, the bigger the problems you can have with cash flow.

To really understand how your stock is working for – or against – you, you need to look honestly at what's actually selling and what isn't.

Start by listing every product or SKU (stock-keeping unit) you sell, along with the number of units sold in the last 12 months (or as long as you have reliable data).

Sort your list by units sold, from highest to lowest:

- The top 20% of products (by sales) are your 'head'
- The bottom 80% are your 'tail', your unproductive stock.

Often, you'll find a long list of products that have only sold a handful of units – or none at all.

Practical exercise

- Make a list of every product/SKU in your business
- Count how many units of each you've sold in the last year

- What percentage of your stock hasn't sold at all in the last 12 months?
- Which products make up the top 20% of sales?
- Which ones make up the rest?

Many business owners are shocked by the results – and by just how much cash is tied up in slow sellers. But when you know what your tail looks like, you can start to shrink it.

Why does the tail matter?

The tail is more than just 'dead' stock. It's an active drain on your business. You pay to buy it, store it, count it and look after it. It also gets in the way, taking up time and space that could be spent on better-selling lines.

Every retailer faces the challenge of managing the tail. But smaller businesses are hit hardest because a small cash flow problem can quickly become a big crisis.

It's hard to let go of stock that you have paid good money for, but the faster your stock turns, the more profitable your business will be. Discounting, running a clearance sale or bundling can help you

Is your stock helping or hurting?

recover some cash – and clear space for lines that will sell better.

How to avoid growing your tail

- Use data to plan new orders – don't buy just to 'fill out' your range
- Set clear rules for when to discount or clear slow-moving lines
- Limit the number of new products you add at any one time
- Focus on re-stocking proven sellers rather than constantly launching new items.

Even if your range is small, building the habit of tracking what's selling (and what isn't), and clearing out the unproductive stock regularly, can mean the difference between success and failure.

So what? Over to you...

1. When did you last look at which of your products are your true bestsellers – and which ones barely sell at all?

Is your stock helping or hurting?

2. Are you holding onto 'tail' stock out of hope, habit or because you 'might' sell it someday?

3. What's one action you could take this week to clear out unproductive stock and put that cash to better use?

Day 5
How much stock do you actually need?

Identifying and managing the tail, which we covered in the previous chapter, is an important part of avoiding your stock building up in the wrong places over time.

One of the other challenges that many businesses face is not knowing how much stock they should even have to begin with. Big businesses have stock limits that they treat very seriously, but most small businesses don't have a stock budget, so when things don't sell or old stock starts to build up, no alarms are sounded. And yet, having too much stock is one of the fundamental reasons that product businesses have problems with their cash flow.

If you create a stock plan, you too can have this monthly focus on whether or not you have the right amount of stock in your business – enough to fulfil sales but not so much that your money is trapped. That will give you a clear number to work towards and help you understand how much you can afford to be holding in stock.

The foundations of good stock planning

1. **Know your sales patterns.** Look at your sales over the past year (or as far back as you can). When are your peaks and troughs?
2. **Set a sales forecast.** Even a rough estimate helps you buy more confidently.
3. **Work out your ideal stock cover.** This is how many weeks or months' worth of stock you want to hold at any one time.
4. **Keep your bestsellers in stock.** Run your numbers to see which lines drive the most profit – and make sure you never run out.
5. **Monitor slow sellers and avoid over-ordering.** The tail can grow quickly if you don't keep an eye on what's not moving.

How much stock do you actually need?

Case study: Emmanuel's stock headaches

One of my big strategies for last year was becoming a 'one-stop shop' for design-loving individuals, and I went out and found lots of fantastic new brands to stock to help me achieve that goal.

With the fulfilment centre move, I was suddenly able to have as many products as I liked – it was like having unlimited space. I got a bit carried away.

My stock is way higher than last year, but then my sales are up too. It's hard to know how to hit the right balance between choice and stock. If I think about my stock as the money it represents instead of physical products, that's quite eye opening. I visited my fulfilment centre yesterday and just walking past the racking of my products was sobering.

After surveying my customers, I decided to pull back on my range – not necessarily discounting them, but I marked them as 'do not reorder' on my master list to help me see easily what I was selling through and not replacing. My plan is to keep selling through these lines and in about six months have a stock clearance sale to mop up anything that hasn't shifted.

You don't have to check your stock daily, but a regular monthly (or at least quarterly) stock check helps you see problems early.

How to set a stock cover target

Think about how quickly you want to turn your stock over – that is, how many weeks or months you want your average product to sit before being sold.

For most small product businesses, two to three months of stock cover is a good target – enough to weather delays, but not so much that your money is stuck.

To calculate your cover:

- Work out your average monthly sales (in units or value)
- Multiply by the number of months' cover you want
- That's the amount of stock (by units or value) you should aim to hold.

For example, if you sell 100 units per month, and want two months' cover, you should aim to have about 200 units in stock at any time. Don't forget to factor in lead times – how long it takes for your supplier to deliver after you place an order. If it takes six weeks to restock, you'll need to order before you run out.

How much stock do you actually need?

Avoid the 'feast and famine' cycle

Many small businesses buy in large batches when cash allows, then go through a cycle of feast and famine: loads of stock at once, then long stretches of selling down and worrying about running out.

Regular, smaller orders (where possible) smooth out cash flow and keep your range fresh.

When it comes to new products or launches:

- Start with a small quantity
- See how it sells
- Be prepared to reorder quickly if it takes off – but avoid overcommitting until you have data.

Making stock decisions with confidence

A good stock plan is a living document, not a one-time task. Review and adjust as your business changes:

- Review your sales regularly – which products are growing, and which are slowing?
- Adjust your stock cover target for peak and quiet periods.
- Don't be afraid to change suppliers or drop products that don't perform.

So what? Over to you...

1. When did you last review your stock levels and sales data side by side?

How much stock do you actually need?

2. Are you ordering 'just in case' or based on clear patterns and targets?

3. What is one thing you could do this month to make your stock planning more confident and less stressful?

Day 6
What does it cost to stay open?

Every product business, whether thriving or just scraping by, faces the same crucial question: what does it really cost just to keep the doors open? Understanding your 'stomach' – the essential costs that must be covered before a single penny of profit appears – is a key step to taming your tiger business. Today's focus is on break-even analysis, fixed versus variable costs and the peace of mind that comes from knowing your numbers.

Knowing exactly how much money you need to keep your business going every month is incredibly freeing. As a business grows, costs seem to multiply: rent, salaries, utilities, insurance, marketing – each one demands its bite. So, how do you get a grip on what your minimum sales need to be just to keep the tiger fed, but not starving you in the process?

Many business owners avoid looking at these numbers because they're worried about what they'll find. However, in my experience, those who know exactly what they're dealing with feel more empowered, less anxious and are better able to make decisions based on facts, not fears.

What is a break-even analysis?

A break-even analysis is one of the most valuable calculations you can do for your product business. In short, it tells you the amount of sales you need to cover all your costs – after that, any further sales are profit. This number is not about wishful thinking or ambitious targets but about basic survival.

Identifying your fixed and variable costs

Before you can calculate your break-even point, you need to know what your costs are. This is where many people get stuck. The key is to break down your costs into two categories.

What does it cost to stay open?

Fixed costs

Fixed costs are the costs that you pay regardless of whether you make one sale or a hundred. These include things like rent, salaries, website hosting, insurance and subscriptions. They do not vary according to how much you sell – if you took a holiday for a month and made no sales, you would still have to pay these costs.

Variable costs

Variable costs, on the other hand, are costs that only occur when you make a sale. For example, the cost of buying your products, packaging, postage, transaction fees – these all go up or down depending on how many sales you make. If you make no sales, you don't pay any variable costs.

Many product businesses make the mistake of confusing the two or trying to average them together. It's much more useful to list them separately. The more specific you can be with your fixed and variable costs, the more accurate your break-even number will be. Don't guess or estimate – go through your last three months' bank statements and list every regular outgoing.

Getting clear on your numbers

Let's look at some examples.

Salma the shop owner's fixed costs each month include shop rent, business rates, utilities, staff wages, insurance and her website hosting fee. Her variable costs are the price she pays to suppliers for each item, packaging and payment processing fees.

Emmanuel the e-commerce seller's fixed costs include his fulfilment centre's monthly fee, website subscriptions, accounting software and insurance. His variable costs are the cost of each product, shipping to customers and payment fees.

Irene the illustrator's fixed costs include her studio rent, subscriptions for design software and a part-time assistant's wages. Her variable costs are the cost of printing each card or print, envelopes, packaging and the postage on each order.

Calculating your break-even point

Once you've split your costs, it's time to calculate what sales you need to break even. Here's the basic formula:

Break-even sales = Fixed costs ÷ (Average % margin)

First, total up your monthly fixed costs.

What does it cost to stay open?

Next, you need to know your average margin. This is the average percentage you keep from each sale after deducting the direct costs (cost of product, packaging, postage, etc) – in other words, your gross profit margin.

For example: if your fixed costs are £2,000 per month and your average margin is 60% (i.e. you keep 60p from every £1 sold after deducting variable costs), then your break-even sales are: £2,000 ÷ 0.6 = £3,333

So, you need to make £3,333 in sales each month just to break even.

This is a powerful number. It tells you the reality of what you need to achieve. If you're consistently below it, you're running at a loss; if you're above, you're making a profit.

(NB if you are VAT registered, remember to remove VAT from your sales before you calculate your margin and break-even. The same applies for fixed costs – remove any VAT that you can reclaim, so you're only looking at real costs.)

If your business is seasonal (e.g. you do most of your sales at Christmas), you may want to calculate your break-even over a year rather than a month. Spread your fixed costs over twelve months and see what the average monthly break-even looks like.

Common pitfalls and how to avoid them

- **Ignoring small costs.** Little things add up. Don't ignore 'minor' costs like software subscriptions, bank fees or small regular purchases.
- **Using unrealistic margins.** Be honest about your margins. Use your actual numbers, not what you wish they were.
- **Forgetting to update costs.** Your costs will change over time. Review your fixed and variable costs every few months to make sure your break-even analysis is still accurate.

What does this mean for your business?

Knowing your break-even sales figure gives you clarity. You can use this number to set realistic sales targets, make informed decisions about spending and plan for growth. If your break-even point is higher than your current average sales, that's a clear signal that you need to either increase sales, cut costs, or both.

If you're consistently comfortably above break-even, you might be ready to invest in growth – new products, marketing, staff.

What does it cost to stay open?

What if you don't like the number?

It's normal to feel daunted by your break-even sales target, especially if it's higher than you expected. But now that you know the number, you can do something about it. You can focus on:

- **Increasing your margin.** Can you raise prices, cut costs or sell more high-margin products?
- **Reducing your fixed costs.** Are there any subscriptions, services or expenses you can cut or renegotiate?
- **Growing your sales.** What can you do to increase your sales above the break-even point?

Case study reflections

Salma was shocked when she first calculated her break-even sales and saw how much her shop needed to make each month. But after the initial panic, she was able to use that information to make decisions – cutting unnecessary expenses, focusing her marketing and making sure her bestsellers were always in stock.

Emmanuel realized he was just barely covering his costs during quieter months. By digging into his break-even numbers, he identified opportunities to streamline his fulfilment process and negotiate better rates with suppliers.

Irene found her break-even was lower than she'd feared, giving her the confidence to invest in new product lines.

What does it cost to stay open?

 So what? Over to you…

1. What are your actual fixed costs each month – and is there anything you could reduce, renegotiate or eliminate to bring your break-even down?

2. How does your average gross margin compare to your target margin? Are you using real numbers or best guesses?

What does it cost to stay open?

3. How will knowing your break-even sales target change the way you plan your business, your goals or your pricing going forward?

Day 7
How can you grow without burning out?

Managing costs is important, but the way to long-term success ultimately lies through growth, and now you understand how to control your tiger, you're in a great place to think about your sales plan. You might be surprised how many ways there are to grow revenue profitably and sustainably, without sending your stress levels through the roof.

Four ways to grow your sales

1. Get more customers
2. Increase your conversion rate

How can you grow without burning out?

3. Get each customer to spend more
4. Get customers to buy more often

Let's look at each one.

1. Get more customers

This is the growth path that most business owners think of first: getting more people to buy from you. This can mean attracting new customers to your online store, getting new footfall into your shop or opening up new wholesale accounts. For this strategy, you might think about social media marketing, paid advertising, PR, collaborations and partnerships, events, new sales channels and so on.

But the reality is that acquiring new customers is often the most expensive way to grow. Getting a steady stream of new traffic onto your site or through your doors should absolutely be a key priority, but it's expensive and time consuming to constantly be speaking to people who don't know you. It's like hosting a party but spending all your time trying to persuade more people to join you, instead of focusing on the guests who have already arrived. So think too about the other, perhaps more sustainable, ways to grow...

2. Increase your conversion rate

If you can improve your conversion rate, your sales will grow without the need for more followers or the need to spend more money on advertising.

To calculate your conversion rate, divide the number of sales you have in a certain period (for example, the last week or last month) by the number of visitors in that period:

Conversion rate = number of transactions/ number of visitors expressed as a percentage

So, if you sell two items in a week and have 100 visitors, you have a 2% conversion rate (2/100, expressed as a percentage). The typical conversion rate for an e-commerce site is around 2%. A physical space will usually be higher, around 25–50%.

The time and effort you spend on improving your conversion rate will pay big dividends, as it allows you to turn people who are already interested into paying customers. For an online store, think about the quality and usefulness of your photographs, how much information is available, the ease of purchasing and so on. Offline, think about your store layout and the way you greet customers. And for both, it's all about the desirability, freshness and distinctiveness of your products.

3. Get each customer to spend more

Another way to drive sales that is often overlooked is measuring and increasing the average transaction value (ATV), also known as average basket size. This is a very profitable way to grow as it requires no additional customers or marketing.

ATV = total sales value of your orders/number of orders placed

For example, if your sales were £300 across five orders, your ATV is £300/5 = £60. If you can increase the amount spent by each customer to £66, your sales will increase by 10% without the need to get any more customers.

Small changes – bundling, encouraging people to buy a set instead of a single product, suggesting low-price 'add-on' items at checkout or offering free shipping over a certain spend – can have a significant effect on your ATV. Look for ways to 'trade up' your customers, making it easy and attractive for them to spend a little more each time.

4. Get customers to buy more often

The final method to grow your sales is to get your existing customers to buy more often, or how you nurture your customers to keep them engaged.

Are you reaching out to people who have bought from you previously for feedback? Are you encouraging them to take a look at your new products? You have a much higher chance of converting a previous customer than converting someone who is coming across your brand for the first time.

This is where email marketing is important. Are you tagging customers when they make a potentially recurring purchase, such as a yearly diary, so that you can target them with a follow-up? Do you know who your VIP/most frequent customers are, and do you have a special loyalty scheme for them? These are the people who pay your bills, so why not take ten minutes to brainstorm how you can keep them happy?

Repeat customers are generally much better customers all round. They tend to return fewer items, spend more and are much more likely to complete reviews or feedback and advocate for your brand. They are well worth your time and attention.

Putting it all together: your sales strategy

A well-thought-out sales strategy coupled with a strong understanding of your key numbers is

How can you grow without burning out?

important when it comes to growing your business in a way that feels controlled.

Successful product businesses do not just measure how many new customers they are getting each month; they focus on growing sales through all four areas. If you do the same, you will not only increase your topline sales, but your profits will grow too.

You may also find that having a broad range of strategies to grow your sales will help, over time, to create more consistent sales for your business. If you are solely reliant on one tactic, such as social media, to bring in new customers, then if you have issues with that platform it can impact your whole business. Diversified ways of growing sales can help even out the highs and lows.

Creating a business that is growing profitably is about much more than trying to get more people through the door or onto the website. It's about creating a sales strategy that takes into consideration all of the different ways to grow.

The most effective growth strategies are the ones that play to your strengths, suit your stage of business and feel sustainable for you. You don't have to do it all. Focus on what works and be willing to experiment.

Grow Your Product Business

Smart, sustainable growth is about knowing your numbers, understanding your customers and making choices that support your business and your wellbeing. You are the expert in your own business. Listen to your gut, track your numbers and take small, intentional steps. Growth is possible, and it can be joyful, not exhausting.

How can you grow without burning out?

✏️ So what? Over to you...

1. What would it mean to you to grow your business sustainably?

2. Which of the four ways to grow sales feels most relevant to your business right now, and why?

How can you grow without burning out?

3. What small, specific experiment can you run this week to put that in hand?

Day 8
Are you charging enough?

Pricing is part numbers, part nerve. Getting your prices right is not just about maths – it's about confidence, clarity and believing in the value you provide. The right price underpins your business's health and your own sense of self-worth as a business owner.

Don't assume that you'll only make a sale if you charge less for your products. If you underprice your products significantly, you can affect how your customers think about your products. Pricing inadvertently reflects your beliefs about yourself and your business. Subconsciously, pricing challenges your thoughts about money and what you think you can charge for different products. You've got to try and set a price that makes you feel comfortable. Working out the price is part art and part science but there are a few basic principles that are important to apply.

The three-step pricing process

The best approach is to work through a logical process to ensure that your prices are correct for your customer and your competitive market. Once you have done these exercises, then you can check your profitability.

Step 1: Learn from competitors

No business operates in isolation, so be aware of the market price for your products. The first step when it comes to setting your prices is to analyse what your competitors are doing. Look at their pricing to help you build a benchmark for your own product pricing.

The trap that many small businesses fall into here is that they compare themselves to the wrong kind of competitor. They look at a big supermarket and see that they sell a T-shirt for £5 and wonder how they can compete with that price. The simple answer? They can't. But that's OK. People have many reasons for buying from supermarkets, just like they have different reasons for buying from small businesses.

Setting your prices compared to competitors requires looking at people who share a similar business model to you. If you hand-pour your soy wax candles, look for three other businesses that do the same. If your clothes are made from organic cotton in a small factory in Portugal, who else does that? However, once you have found the correct competitors to give you a comparison you don't have to match their prices exactly. You can have your own pricing and it can even be a point of differentiation between you and your competition.

(NB If you haven't checked your competitors' pricing recently, it's worth another look. When prices are rising, it's especially important to keep your competitor information updated.)

Step 2: Ask your customers

The next step after reviewing your competitors' prices is to make sure that you are cross-referencing what your customers typically pay. If you say, 'Would you pay £125 for this T-shirt?' they are likely to answer 'Yes', but if you ask them 'How much were the last three T-shirts you bought?' and they say £20–£25, then you have a better idea of the real prices they are prepared to pay.

Are you charging enough?

Consistent feedback from genuine customers that your prices are too high is important information; random comments from the odd stranger who will probably never buy from you anyway is not. There's no price low enough for a critic.

Step 3: Avoid pricing pitfalls

Pay attention to psychological price points such as £10, £20, £50 or £100. For example, it's much better to price at £99 than £102. One is under £100, and one has gone over that psychological barrier.

Avoid 'odd' and inconsistent prices. Try and streamline the number of different price points that you use. If you have items at £12, £13 and £14, can you just group them together at one price point? The clearer and easier your price architecture is, the less confusion there will be in the mind of your customer.

Testing and adjusting your prices

Ultimately, your customer will dictate your pricing. You can spend hours theorizing over the best price points, but it's better just to set your prices and start selling. You can always adjust prices, although I suggest leaving four to six weeks before changing anything so that you have time to review your sales.

If you're selling very little, don't immediately assume that this means your prices are too high, unless you know for a fact that you are considerably more expensive than your immediate competitors (e.g. those of a similar quality to you). Customers make assumptions about your product based on the price, so if you've priced too low, they might assume your quality is lacking. On the flip side, if you are selling an item very quickly (faster than you can get it back into stock, for example) then this is usually a sign that there is room to increase your prices.

Raising prices: overcoming fear and communicating change

One of the biggest barriers to people raising their prices is the worry over what people will say. In reality, very few customers will even notice.

Some people prefer to let their customers know about a price change. This can be a good way to build trust and communication between you and your customers. In this case, you would inform people that on X date prices will be increasing, and if they want to purchase beforehand, they'll be able to take advantage of the existing price. This is often a nice way to encourage sales. If you sell at wholesale, you'd

Are you charging enough?

also be able to inform your stockists of your plans and encourage them to purchase from you before the deadline. Other people prefer to not draw attention to the price increase and that is equally valid.

Either way, it is often helpful to have some pre-written responses just in case you do get a customer complaint. For example:

> *Thank you so much for being a repeat customer, I appreciate your custom. Thank you for your comments regarding the increased price. I recently completed a business review and due to rising costs have had to pass on a small portion of the price increase to the customer in order to stay competitive.*
>
> *I do appreciate that you purchased at a lower price last time. In which case, I would like to offer you a 10% discount on your next order to thank you for your loyalty.*

Having this pre-written can be hugely helpful as you go about the task of reviewing and potentially reworking your prices.

Your pricing should reflect the reality of what your business needs, not just your nerves. There is no shame in charging what you need to charge to run a profitable, sustainable business. The right customers will value what you do.

So what? Over to you…

1. When was the last time you compared your pricing to competitors selling similar products and business models? What did you discover?

Are you charging enough?

2. How confident do you feel about communicating a price increase to your customers if your costs go up? What message would you want them to hear?

3. Does your current pricing support the business – and life – you want, or are you leaving money on the table? What's your next step?

Day 9
How do you fix slim margins?

What happens if you run your numbers only to discover that your margins are not that great? This is a common situation that many small business owners find themselves in. But there are practical fixes – from negotiating costs to smarter bundling – that can make a big difference to your profits.

Six strategies for fixing slim margins

1. Negotiating with suppliers

If you work with a particular supplier, especially if you have done so for a few months or longer, it may well be worth speaking to them about your pricing. One of the most effective ways of doing this is framing your question in the following way: 'I have been reviewing my margins, and in an ideal world I'd be paying X for this item. What would it take for me to get that price?' Sometimes the answer will be that they can't ever accommodate that price. Sometimes they'll give you options.

It's sometimes possible to negotiate a better deal if you commit to a certain amount. You don't always have to take all of that stock at the same time; it could be a firm commitment to take that amount across the whole year is enough for them to agree to give you a better price. Maybe they'll give you a better price if you pay upfront (if you're not paying upfront already). Sometimes they might make suggestions on how you can tweak the product in order to bring it in at the price you want it to be.

However, use your judgement carefully. If they are offering a better price per unit for larger quantities, it may not be the right decision for you to take it. You should always balance lower costs per unit against the impact that this will have on your cash flow, not to mention the difficulties that might arise in storing extra products! Another factor to consider is how long it takes to sell that amount of stock. If you think that you could clear that amount in a few months,

How do you fix slim margins?

that's one thing. But buying years' worth of stock just to get a better unit price is not ideal.

2. Cross-costing

Cross-costing is the retail term for price checking against different suppliers. It's a worthwhile exercise, even if you are happy with your current supplier. It also helps avoid having all your eggs in one supplier basket. If you have low margins because the product, or one of the elements of your product, is too expensive, it's definitely worth taking the time to get quotes from other suppliers. Even if you remain with your existing supplier, the best time to find an alternative supplier is when you are not in urgent need.

3. Blended margins and bundling

If you have certain products that are strong sellers but have poor margins, is it possible to combine them together with other items to give you a better overall margin? This is known as a blended margin, and it can be a useful way to push up the profitability in your business. Let's say Emmanuel has a beautiful tea towel that he sells in his shop. It is very popular but because of the way it is made (hand-dyed in India and then embroidered), it's expensive for him to buy in. Emmanuel decides to combine this tea towel with a set of his stainless-steel food containers (high margin) to create a gift set that is on average in his target margin range.

4. Reverse engineering pricing

If you're happy with your prices but the profits aren't high enough, ask yourself if there is anything you can do to reverse engineer items into a better profit margin. Let's say that Irene is going to sell a cushion for £75, she is VAT registered and wants to achieve a 65% margin.

She calculates that her target cost price is:

Target cost price (20% VAT-registered businesses) = (retail price/1.2) × (1 − ideal margin)
(£75/1.2) × (1−65%) = £62.50 × 35% = £21.88

Imagine she gets a quote from a supplier for a cushion with tassels and piping, silk backing and hand embroidery picking out elements of the design for £29 per cushion.

With a target cost price in mind, she can work with the supplier to understand what could be removed from the product. What's the price without the tassels? Is there a cheaper way to finish the edges? What if instead of silk she used cotton? How much would it cost to reduce or remove the embroidery?

The supplier will not, in general, be offended by these types of questions. These are the types of discussions that happen hundreds of times a day in big retailers. Just make sure that you aren't impacting the quality of the product, and you aren't removing something that makes you unique or is part of your business DNA.

For example, if your entire business is built on an ethos of minimizing your environmental impact and supporting organic cotton, it's no good switching your organic cotton for standard cotton.

Focusing on your pricing and then working into the cost price will help you home in on where you can cut costs but still offer your customer something they want.

5. First price, right price

You'll notice that so far I haven't mentioned anything about raising prices if your margins aren't high enough. That's because it should be your last resort after looking at every other way to improve your in-margin. Having said that, part of having an effective profitable business does rely on you being on top of your pricing and being aware of competitors. See Day 8 for more on this!

6. Monitoring and maintaining margins

The best margin improvements come from small, regular checks. Keep a close eye on your biggest costs. Regularly review your product costs, packaging, postage and fulfilment. Notice what is creeping up. Act quickly – don't just absorb the extra cost. Even a 2–3% margin improvement across your range can add up to a significant profit difference over the year.

How do you fix slim margins?

So what? Over to you…

1. Which margin-improving action feels most possible for you right now, and why?

2. What's one small experiment you can run this week to improve your margin?

How do you fix slim margins?

3. How can you monitor and maintain your margins more consistently going forward, rather than waiting until they become a problem?

Day 10
What's next?

You've worked through the numbers, tamed your tiger and you now have clarity on profit, costs, stock and pricing. But how do you keep up momentum – and stay profitable for the long run? This final chapter is about creating a clear, repeatable process to track your progress and continually improve.

Building your retail rhythm

Becoming a tiger tamer is not a one-time event. It is an ongoing process, a set of habits and routines that keep you in control, confident and able to weather the ups and downs of retail. Product businesses are always changing, and so the discipline comes in returning to these numbers regularly.

What's next?

The most successful businesses I work with are the ones who make time to check in with their numbers, who see the data as a tool – not a stick to beat themselves with. They understand that things will fluctuate, but they look at their figures regularly and take action early, before small issues become major headaches.

The tiger tamer's toolkit: your monthly check-in

At the heart of your ongoing process is the monthly check-in – a simple but powerful way to keep your finger on the pulse of your business.

Here's a suggested checklist for your monthly retail review:

- Review your sales – total, by channel and by product
- Check your margins – what's changed, what's slipping?
- Look at your stock levels – what's selling, what's not and where is your cash tied up?
- Track your expenses – any new costs or opportunities to save?
- Monitor cash flow – do you have enough to cover next month's commitments?

- Review your break-even – does it need updating with new numbers?
- Set one or two clear actions for the month ahead.

It doesn't have to take long – set aside 30–60 minutes a month. The key is to make it a non-negotiable habit. The more often you do it, the easier and less scary it becomes.

It's easy to lose sight of how far you've come. One of my favourite tips is to keep a record – a simple spreadsheet or notebook – of key numbers each month. Look back after six months or a year, and you'll see trends, growth and areas that need your attention. Celebrate your wins, however small. Profitability is built on small, consistent improvements over time.

Remember too that life and business are unpredictable. There will be times when you fall behind, miss a review or feel overwhelmed. That's normal. The important thing is to come back to your numbers as soon as you can. Don't let guilt or avoidance build up – every month is a fresh start.

When to get help

You don't have to do this all alone. If you find yourself getting stuck, or need support, consider reaching out – a business mentor, accountant or a supportive business community can make a huge difference. Sometimes just talking your numbers through with someone else gives you a new perspective and helps you move forward.

If you do nothing else…

For those moments when everything feels too much, or if you need to return to basics, these are the elements that I consider to be the bare minimum to feel comfortable and less stressed out by your tiger.

Check your margins

Even if creating the analysis for your net profit margin (see Day 3) feels too time consuming, you must check your gross profit margin to make sure that you are making money on your sales (see Day 2). At the absolute bare minimum, before agreeing to sell something through your business, make sure it is making 50% margin when bought in from another business, and if you intend to sell it on via wholesale, it will need to be at least 65–70% margin.

Most importantly, know what your current average gross profit margin is and keep looking at ways to improve that. Don't forget to keep these numbers up to date as prices increase – I suggest updating your profit margins at least once a quarter.

Know your break-even

Having a strong understanding of what sales are required to cover your fixed costs, based on your net profit margin and your average sales, is one of the most powerful numbers you can know as a business owner. Even if you have to do it based on an estimate of your net profit margin, work it through using the format we explored in Day 6 so that you have that break-even number firmly in your mind.

Watch your stock

If the only thing that you recall from this entire book is the phrase 'the bigger the tail, the bigger the tiger', then I'll be satisfied. Too much underproductive stock creating pockets of trapped cash is one of the most dangerous things that can happen to a product business.

Knowing, at the absolutely bare minimum, how much stock you have and avoiding it piling up is crucial. If this is your focus, refer to Day 4 for more detail.

What's next?

Final thoughts

Retail is always changing, but the principles in this book don't. They have guided businesses of every size through tough times and boom years. Whenever you feel lost or unsure, come back to your numbers – they are your anchor.

Most of all, know that you are not alone. Every product business owner faces challenges. What matters is taking action, little by little, learning as you go, and believing that you can tame your tiger – one step at a time.

So what? Over to you…

1. How will you make reviewing your key numbers a regular, non-negotiable part of your business routine?

What's next?

2. What simple system could you use to track your progress and spot trends – spreadsheet, notebook or something else?

3. Who can you reach out to for support or accountability when you feel stuck or need a fresh perspective?

Conclusion

You've reached the end of this journey, but in many ways this is just the beginning. Taming your tiger isn't about finding a single answer or reaching a final destination – it's about equipping yourself with the tools, habits and mindset to navigate the ever-changing landscape of your product business with confidence and clarity.

Running a product business can be exhilarating, but it can also be overwhelming, lonely and exhausting. The truth is, every business – no matter how established – faces tough months, unexpected costs and moments of doubt. But you are not alone. The experiences shared in this book reflect hundreds of conversations with real business owners, each with their own wins and worries. If you see yourself in their stories, take heart: you have everything you need to thrive.

The most important lesson is this: profit isn't luck, and it isn't magic. It comes from understanding your numbers, asking the right questions and taking regular action. You've learned how to see through the illusion of sales and focus on real profit. You know how to track your costs, measure your margins and manage your stock with intention. You understand the difference between busy-ness and business, and you're ready to make decisions based on fact, not fear.

No one expects you to remember every calculation or to enjoy every spreadsheet. What matters is that you know where to look and what to ask. You know which levers to pull when profits are tight, and you understand how to create sustainable growth without burning out. If there's one thing to carry forward, it's the value of regular review – a monthly check-in with your sales, margins, stock and expenses, so you can course-correct before problems grow.

It's easy to feel pressure to do more, to keep growing, to compare yourself to bigger businesses or louder voices. But growth is only meaningful if it serves *your* goals and values. There is power in knowing your own numbers, your own limits and your own ambitions. Whether you choose to scale up, maintain or pivot, the tools you've practised here will support you at every stage.

Along the way, be kind to yourself. There will be months when you fall behind or feel lost. That's natural. What matters is returning to your numbers and using them as a guide, not a source of shame.

Conclusion

Remember, even small improvements – negotiating a better deal, raising a price, clearing slow stock – can transform your profit over time.

Above all, remember why you started. Your creativity, your passion, your drive to make and sell something special – that's what sets your business apart. These numbers and strategies are here to serve your vision, not limit it. Profitability and purpose are not opposites – they are partners.

Thank you for investing the time and energy to work on your business, not just in it. By building these habits, you are giving yourself the best possible chance – not only of surviving, but of thriving, on your own terms.

Here's to you and to a business you feel proud of. You are the tiger tamer now.

Enjoyed this?
Then you'll love…

Tame Your Tiger by Catherine Erdly

Does your product business feel unpredictable, slightly terrifying and hungry for money? If so, you're not alone.

Retail is the fastest growing small business sector, and for good reason. With accessible selling technology and billions of people shopping online, reaching your ideal customer is easier than ever before.

But the truth is that making money in a product business is harder than it first appears. And without profits, your business becomes incredibly difficult to manage and almost impossible to grow.

Fortunately for you, big retailers have spent decades developing methods of monitoring profit margins, forecasting and growing sales and managing stock to maximize their bottom line.

In this book, small-business retail expert Catherine Erdly shows you how to easily apply those big business tools and perspectives to understand your business, get clear on what you need to do to grow profitably, and, ultimately, tame your tiger.

Other *6-Minute Smarts* titles

 *Beating Burnout* (based on *The Burnout Bible* by Rachel Philpotts)

 *Building Great Teams* (based on *Workshop Culture* by Alison Coward)

 *Collaborate Better* (based on *Collabor(h)ate* by Deb Mashek PhD)

 *Customer Success Essentials* (based on *The Customer Success Pioneer* by Kellie Lucas)

 *Do Change Better* (based on *How to be a Change Superhero* by Lucinda Carney)

 *Find Your Confidence* (based on *Coach Yourself Confident* by Julie Smith)

 *Find Your Purpose* (based on *The Purpose Handbook* by Eloise Skinner)

 *Get That Promotion* (based on *Getting On* by Joanna Gaudoin)

 *How to be Happy at Work* (based on *My Job Isn't Working!* by Michael Brown)

 *How to Get to Know Your Customer* (based on *Do Penguins Eat Peaches?* by Katie Tucker)

 *The Inclusion Mindset* (based on *Beyond Discomfort* by Nadia Nagamootoo)

 *The Listening Leader* (based on *The Listening Shift* by Janie Van Hool)

 *Love Your Job* (based on *WorkJoy* by Beth Stallwood)

 *Managing Big Teams* (based on *Big Teams* by Tony Llewellyn)

 *Mastering People Management* (based on *Mission: To Manage* by Marianne Page)

 *No-Fluff Soft Skills* (based on *Soft Skills, Hard Results* by Anne Taylor)

 *No Nonsense PR* (based on *Hype Yourself* by Lucy Werner)

 *Present Like a Pro* (based on *Executive Presentations* by Jacqui Harper)

 Reimagine Your Career (based on *Work/Life Flywheel* by Ollie Henderson)

 Sales Made Simple (based on *More Sales Please* by Sara Nasser Dalrymple)

The Speed Storytelling Toolkit (based on *Exposure* by Felicity Cowie)

Stay Focused (based on *Attention!* by Rob Hatch)

Write to Think (based on *Exploratory Writing* by Alison Jones)

Look out for more titles coming soon! Visit www.practicalinspiration.com for all our latest titles.

www.ingramcontent.com/pod-product-compliance
Lightning Source LLC
Chambersburg PA
CBHW031433210526
45464CB00005B/2188